Cry Love
Verse II: More New Voices
Edited By Mike O'Connell

First Edition
1 2 3 4 5 6 7 8 9 10

ISBN
13: 978-0692392409
10: 0692392408

Credits
Cover Design: Capooter
Author Frontispieces: Various Artists
ArtArtistsists

Hibernian Publishing, LLC
New Jersey

Dedication

I would like to dedicate this book to all aspiring artists. Whether they be writers, musicians, poets, artists, or actors. They continue to let us know that there are voices to tell the stories of our time. It is these brave individuals who dare to unwrap their souls.

Table of Contents

Damsel in Distress

Kicked

Ashley Rockhill

Two years.

I meticulously ticked-off
Every
Day
on the calendar.

Every minor victory.
Every twitch.
Every ache.
Every longing.

Two years.

And then: a thought –

with the strength of
seven hundred and thirty
successes, I took the bait.
Plunge.
Headfirst.

One.

Tiny.

Taste.

A celebration of success, is all.
Two years;
practically a lifetime.

It felt
like a Lifetime.

That was six years ago.

Seven hundred and thirty
days of hope.
One thousand eight hundred and twenty-seven
affirmations of life.

The difference indistinguishable
in the solitude of my bedroom.

And although I don't mark the calendar –
although I'm alone –
I'm not a failure.

I have two years of success.
So I will keep celebrating.
And remember fondly, those

two

wonderful

years

Baby Steps
Ashley Rockhill

Hold Daddy's hand
learn to walk
Watch his lips
Listen to his words
learn to speak
Stand on his feet
learn to dance
learn to tie
a shoe, a necktie
Watch him make your spaghetti
learn to cook
Let Daddy teach you
to ride a bike
learn to remove
the training wheels
to change a tire
to pump your gas
check the oil
Watch him read the paper
learn to make strong coffee
for bright mornings
after late nights
Hear him come home
at two in the morning
Smell his breath
learn a habit
Watch him
as you grow
into his shoes
learning how to
mask the smell
of whiskey
with perfume

become aloof
to the smell of
beer and cigarettes
clinging to skin
over bruises
under clothes
learn to grow up
just like Daddy

With Love, From Berkley
Ashley Rockhill

A box of bandages
sealed in scar tissue
calloused and coarse
ripped open by screams
in dreams that time
cannot fade
wounds too deep to
fully close

a firecracker
with the force and flash
to bring back the dead
buried in bunkers and foxholes
and darkened dirt tunnels
cities and civilizations
beneath a forest floor
littered with
broken bamboo
bullet casings

return to empty glasses
abandoned bar stools
bottles who understand
people who do not.

Nightmare
Ashley Rockhill

My reflection is strange.
and I stare
and I stare
and I stare
but it doesn't change its shape
but that blood on my hands
won't wash away,
dragging itself
down my face
creeping up my arms
I'm drenched
in someone's blood
clinging and oozing
beneath my clothes
and screaming pierces
the air around me
it's piteous
it's agony
it's wailing
and an angel whispers
what I forgot and
reaching out to touch
it vanishes
like snowflakes and ash
filling my lungs
with grime
I am lost
and I scream
and I scream
and I scream

Street Corners

Ashley Rockhill

my dealer is an older man

graying hair, glasses,

rather unremarkable at best

slightly overweight from over indulgence

me, wasting away to nothing.

I walk into his room

his office he calls it

clean, almost sterile

with its worn carpet

he asks how I am as if

it mattered and I walk out

forty minutes later with

a crumpled slip

blue with barely legible lines

that tells the pharmacist

to give me my fix

Wino

Ashley Rockhill

Ten of thirteen-
named for a bottle
from a long line of drunks.
Johnny Walker, Jim Beam
son begotten
James Walker,
call me Jim.

Depression brew
bottled 1920
saved in lesser years
popped like champagne
for the Second World War
bullets cracked like corks
for a thousand
eighteen, nineteen
somethings
that never left
the Harbor.

Operator---?
can you hear me?
I'd like to make a call.
Thank you. I'll hold.
Operator ---? Valeria --- ?
I'd like to see you.
Would you meet me somewhere?
Please?

Dial tones
were wedding bells
and fifty years
slipped past like

long summer days
and winter nights
bursting with bickering
and laughter:
children, grandchildren

Val --- ?
When is her birthday?
I can't remember.
Don't chastise me,
the kids are coming.
Of course I know they
were here yesterday,
but they're coming today.
Just wait. I'll be outside, Val.

Decades of stories
and bruises and bumped knees
kissed away, smeared with iodine
sneaking to the shed
marking bottles by the day
clouding over things forgotten

Val --- ?
can you hear me?
Fifty-six years
I don't know what to do
The mail pours in
but I don't know
what they want
God won't answer me.
Operator ---Val?
where are you?

Splitting from the rest
like paint peeling
off the rusty trailer,

a new home.
Shutting out the world,
looking through broken mirrors
behind a TV set
watching her favorite show
over and over
forgetting the phone.

Sixty years, it's so cold
Val---are you coming home?
The bottle slipped
I'm not so cold anymore.
Val---who are all these people?
Why are they here?

Trapped by four white walls
and speckled-tile hallways
with a man in the next room
and a name that slips my mind.
My own name slips my mind.
This place is unnerving
sending chills that run deeper
than the bone numbing
echo behind the walls
when the man next door moans.

Ghosts drift down the halls;
sometimes they still have skin
and haven't stopped walking
some are long gone
Val --- ?
Can you hear me?
Where are you?
I'm scared, Val ---

Surgeons sliced open
a wine-soaked abdomen
ripping out the source
of chronic kidney malfunction
closing up the wound
like patching holes in cloth,
punctured skin
looking more grotesque
than the movies depict.

Val ---?
Where is your seam ripper?
I can't find it anywhere
in this damn closet.
When did it get so small?
I tried to take it out
but I must have pricked my finger
Everything is red, Val ---
I'm dizzy and I need you
I think I hit my head.
Val? Is that really you?

Ambivalence
Ashley Rockhill

They tell me I have a disease
sitting in this God-forsaken circle
established in 1935
when Depression ran high, poison
back on the market.
I have my scapegoat now
my own personal excuse
because I'm not well.
Sick. Diseased.
But I'm feeling okay,
with my whiskey hangover.

Crossfire
Ashley Rockhill

Someone's been shot.

I'm not sure who.

I ran for help
sweat running down my neck
pitching a cigarette
onto a lawn of Solo cups

Stumble up the steps
head pounding
begging those in earshot
to call an ambulance

head in my hands
   it stings
    hands tinged red

I'm bleeding
for a man
who never pulled a trigger
but ran away

a man like me

Liang Zhu, The Butterfly Lovers

Ashley Rockhill

Cracked and crumbling earth
beneath my nails,
 raked in sorrow and
 under inscribed stone,
earth gives way.

   I join sour soil
   as it opens beneath me.

     But the earth cannot
     devour me.

   With a final sigh as breath fades
   I rise on wings I did not earn.
   I feel an echoed beat to my side.

And we fly away
 to places we could never dream,
 on wings we could never deserve,
to live together changed.

Charming
Ashley Rockhill

You're charming.

I had forgotten that.

Standing with friends
unknowingly shared
I feel my world shrinking.

They introduce us unaware
of past intimacy misspent.
I wait, poised to attack,
waiting for you to strike first.

But you're charming.

And you don't.

And then anger flows out
like venom
spitting out words
bottled inside.

But these friends are new
to each of us
and don't understand.
They just see me

And you.

Being so fucking charming.

Pocket

Ashley Rockhill

surrounded by boxes
   jotting down dreams
   on post-it notes
lists of obligations
   orders to fill
   people to serve
notes crumpled
   into coat pockets
   forgotten and given away
old and wrinkled
   successful, regretful
   it's too late

he cries.

Emperor
Ashley Rockhill

I hate them.

They stand about in clusters
with their pristine suits
and orange trim about their throats.

Their pointed faces and focused eyes
cast sideways glances
that make me squirm from afar.

They usher me away wordlessly
with the only sound a muffled
shuffling of feet across downy carpet.

They delight in the coming crowd
idling with contemptuous indifference
while mulling about their affairs.

The newly arrived are ensnared
captured by their iconic movement
and wooed by their seemingly awkward motion.

One brave soul presents
them offerings of silver
both parties oblivious to the slime.

I stand frozen
unwilling or unable to move
as if trapped in ice.

Because they see me and know.

I know.

I fear.

Words
Ashley Rockhill

She wrote down their words in a notebook.
When she ran out of space, she wrote on her body.
When her body was scarred, she turned it to bone.
When she had nothing left, she picked up a pen
and began anew.

Broken Wings

Ashley Rockhill

I am not a phoenix.
I descend
with wingless plummet
into madness.
Cradled by the glow of defeat,
the roar of self-destruction,
I burn.
Amongst the crackle
with acrid smoke
I embrace agony
with failure's devotion.
Within my pyre
I crumble to ashen dust
with fire dancing around me,
ripping through me,
in its glory and vivacity
leaving nothing but blackened bone.
Amidst the roar of amber flame
and odor of charred flesh,
I hear the sound of wings
rising above me
fanning the fire.
I am not the phoenix.
I return to my blaze.

Toil and Trouble

Diary for Dementia
Andrew Switzer

Intermittent scribbles in a brand new leather journal.
Hoping even just one line becomes something eternal.
Searching for the perfect words, or poignant points to make,
I lay there, thinking, three a.m., and I'm still wide awake.
Pretty rhymes to pass the time, if no soul ever reads,
I write these words for mockingbirds and fun, no thoughts of greed.
The verdant, rolling plains of the space within my skull,
Spill forth in excess on the page when life is feeling dull.
Words give life to drying ink, a pause between each line,
To choose the words which through the years remind me what is mine.

Hold On

Andrew Switzer

Quivering hands as soft as silk,
Skin as white as mother's milk.
Hair the color of sunsets glow,
Gentle as the falling snow.
Outside my window, chilling winds,
Flawless lips form a tremulous grin.
Tangled bodies trap the heat.
Where clothing ends and bare skin meets
Between the mattress and the sheets,
Two bodies sing unsung desires.
Those piercing eyes like emerald fire
Bathe my features in warm affection.
The chance to form a deep connection
Guides a driver without direction.
Demons dwell in lonely nights,
I beg you, please, just hold on tight.

Still

Andrew Switzer

I tell myself I write these words for no specific face,
But I can't lie, to my mind's eye, when placing them on pages
Bound in leather, held together, by the loves I never knew,
Doesn't matter who I flatter, still, I dream of you.
Your name, as sweet as honeysuckle, passes through my lips,
I miss the sin of your silk skin beneath my fingertips.
Thinking thoughts of drinking, drowning memories turned blue,
A million months of nights spent drunk, and still, I dream of you.

Between the Lines

Andrew Switzer

Growing flames will turn your name into a cloud of ashes.
A flowing mane remains untamed through whirling dervish clashes.
Beating hearts as hope departs through valleys long and winding,
Burning sun, you turn and run, the path ahead is blinding.
You always knew I wouldn't do, so why'd you even bother?
Pass my time by penning rhymes and double fisting lagers.

I Want You

Andrew Switzer

I want you to look into my eyes and see shelter from the storm of society and selfishness that smother our spirits and leaves us broken and alone.

I want you to rest your battle beaten body in my warm embrace and know that the wars of yesterday are over. That you can lay down your arms while taking up mine, leaving the attacking forces behind and staying home to defend that to which your heart has been entrusted.

I want you to hear my voice and know that nothing else matters but we two. To know that calmer, gentler times are on the horizon. Times safe from uncertainty and fear, loneliness and solitude.

I want you to accept my hand in yours and know that, from this moment forth, everything will be alright.

One

Andrew Switzer

The world around me slows to a crawl,
No one around me knows me at all.
I look over the crowd of familiar faces,
From various times and different places.
They laugh and they play, one and another,
All with secret pains, I'm just like the others.

Eternal Sleep

Andrew Switzer

Faking structure through the years,
Answers lost in amber beers.
Waking up to each new day,
Hoping I will float away,
High above the reach of man,
His damning, racist, hateful clan.
To a place of deepest night,
Safe from bigots "cleansing light."
Darkness thick as velvet rope
Holds together all my hopes,
And dreams and fears and all desires,
Under stars and nightly fires.
Break away from everyone,
Claim the night, blot out the sun.
When one day the long sleep falls,
I'll journey down those crimson halls,
To crypts of love and memories lost,
Without a care about the cost.

Doesn't Really Matter

Andrew Switzer

Nobody really knows
Which, if any, way the wind blows.
Drifting by on fading dreams,
All for one, no time for teams.
Days gone by when we flew high on vapors not of rolling papers,
But of our playful youthful capers, daring mates as daylight tapers.
Now the times have changed for ill,
When all we praise is Dollar Bill.
Robots set on cruise control,
But what's the purpose, what's the goal?
When the dam will burst at last, cleansing all that was our past,
We'll have the life and riches, too,
But what's the point, when you're not you?

Anatomy of a Break Up

Andrew Switzer

Her hot breath bathes your bare chest in the warmth that nothing else can provide. One hand wrapped around the waist, legs intertwined, she sleeps, her gentle, steady heartbeat as infectious as any melody you've ever known. The only source of light is a flickering candle, casting dancing shadows upon the walls and ceiling. Discarded garments and drained bottles of wine litter the floor, the obvious aftermath of an evening quite certainly well spent.

The stage is set, and the actors are in position. The assembled crowd holds its collective breath, both eager and fearful of how this tale is to end. As our two young lovers sleep deeply, the candle continues to fade, it's once exuberant and animated flame growing ever dimmer, until it fails in a sudden plume of smoke.

On cue, the comely lass springs to life, situating herself to straddle our poor lad. Her auburn hair falls to form a curtain around her suddenly nightmarish features. In one swift movement, she swings the dagger 'round and plunges it deep into his flailing torso. With sickening precision, she reaches in and forcefully removes his still beating heart. She makes her way to the door, the heartbeat fading to a gentle throb as she increases the distance between you, until it disappears into the cool night air.

The curtains fall. Applause. The audience departs, returning to their lives, unaffected by the passionate butchery they've just witnessed. The female lead goes on to enjoy the accolades and affection attended to shooting stars, as our unfortunate male is relegated to the role of bit player. Oh, how I miss the days of dreamless slumber.

2 am

Andrew Switzer

The street lights bathe with golden glow
People passing on roads below.
Where they come from, who they are,
All meaningless, beneath the stars.
But when two people chance to meet,
And share the loves they seldom speak,
They form a bond no test can break,
Love to give is love to make.

The Violet Hour

Andrew Switzer

In this violet hour, as dreams court demons and the seams holding the ocean of your soul threaten to split and spill forth your essence into the sky above, time almost seems to stand still. The space around you becomes skewed as gravity gives way to weightless flight above a world that never made sense to you in the first place. All the pain, persecution, and perils that are inflicted upon such immense portions of the populations of no one single nation, but all races, creeds, and castes, and at the end of the day it all boils down to the search for the almighty dollar. But none of that matters to you anymore. As you are borne on by invisible wings along the waves of the universe, guided towards the boundaries of feeling, you begin to embrace the emptiness that is nothingness. Your once harried mind now free from the chaos of being, unclouded by delusions of grandeur and eternity, you allow yourself all the time you need to enjoy this respite from thought. Time has become meaningless. Eons pass, knowable existence collapsing inwards on itself, only to explode into radiance and vitality once more. The cycle continues, hundreds of times in the space of time necessary to form a few sentences, while at the same time slowing to such a point that galaxies could be traversed in the breadth of a heartbeat. Adrift in the void, with no tether back to the realm of mortals, the only course of action is to allow yourself to be lost to sightless visions and wordless descriptions of an existence that you can no longer remember.

In Shadows

Andrew Switzer

In shadows she cries as the weight of the world consumes her.
No one ever cared; they all seemed to stare right through her.
On the wings of the angels she flies through the skies just to be with him.
Trampled by devils, she's dragged underground as the light grows dim.

Torn into pieces, her soul she unleashes in the crimson flow.
The blades stick fast in the dirt as she gasps in the pale moon glow.
No whimper or whine as she counts down the time till her heart stops
beating.
Her skin grows pale as her life force fails and she welcomes his cold
greeting.

Silence
Andrew Switzer

Bitter winter winds have broken
into biting rains - it's soaking
earthen muck, 'neath unsure footing,
inebriated lush.
As I took my leave of gathered
friends and spirits, nothing mattered.
My farewell you found off-putting,
Saw you start to blush.

The simple act of placing lips
against your tender fingertips
would find you fleeing up the stairs.
Just turn and walk away.
Unspoken token, affection
of a deepening connection.
Not one word said, not one soul cares,
but I can't look away.

I wait and watch you disappear
through the fading smoke and mirrors.
I thought one day you'd call again,
never ending silence
echoes out the only mistake
that I'd ever admit to make,
for on that night I lost a friend.
Self-inflicted silence.

Locks

Lines
Sarah Galo

The air my hands rode, while your lips pouted and read French,
 and loved,

Being called Tracey and Hepburn, marking the division or
 boundary of us,

The tears from my lashes to the hallow of my neck to my navel
 in the barren night,

Sitting still and straight, praying over the light in my hands
 that it may follow you.

When Snow White Wakes Up and Speaks for the First Time

Sarah Gallo

I didn't really die, as everyone assumed. The apple wasn't really poisoned
with cyanide, or whatever the hell will do you in. Just a heavy
dose of Xanax, or was it Lunesta?

Something to relax the body and the mind. You know I was in an awful
tizzy all the time. Running around, manically singing to the birds,
while scrubbing the floor, washing the dishes, making the dinner -

working my ass off for these poor helpless men. They couldn't live, could
hardly breathe till I came along. How or why I got here isn't of
concern. I was sent, you may say. God's gift to men,

to cook, clean make everything pure again, modeled after my own virginal
self. I was tired, damn tired, when the old lady came by. I needed
a break. And she offered the apple, a beautiful shiny apple.

They, the men, had warned me before, *Don't eat the apple. That's why Eve
fell, and Adam too. If anyone strange comes along, ignore them, keep on
with your work (for us), they're after you. They may want to steal your
soul.*

I nodded and smiled, the bobbed black curls bobbing, my nearly
translucent skin blushing. *Take care, Snow White.* Why the hell
they called me that, I do not know, but when this old lady came,
all cold and tired, with this beautiful apple,

that was supposedly the cause of the fall of my kind, and I was promised
eternal beauty and the like, well why the hell not? I thought.
I took the apple, more than took it, I ripped it from her hand,

biting the crisp fruit, my lips puckering from the tartness . . . and I felt
tired. But wonderfully, peacefully tired. *Good night, sweet girl*, said
the old lady. As my body settled into a new state,

I realized my opportunity, sleep, sleep, sleep. Free from the chores, the
obligations and assumptions . . . I don't remember how I ended up
in a glass coffin or how I was kissed awake by a strange man,

who lifted me from my resting place, and tried to help me onto his horse.
What is this? I said, speaking aloud, my voice strangely soft and
whiny – Is this what I sound like? Good Lord,

help me – who are you? Why are you taking me to your castle far away?
Where's the old lady, with her beautiful apples sugar-coated with
Xanax or Lunesta, whatever the hell it was? I don't want to work.

No more scrubbing dishes, no more singing with the birds, no more of this
bobble-head mentality. I won't go with you, or back with those
old bastards. Find me the old lady, I just want to go back to sleep.

When Sleeping Beauty Finds Her Voice On Reality TV
Sarah Galo

"I married My Rapist and Didn't Know It," Coming soon to Lifetime on
    channel fifty-four should follow that. Or shaking and crying as I
    walk onto a sound stage, with Oprah shouting, "And heeeeeere's
    Auroraaaaaa the Sleeeeeepy BEAUUUU-TYY!"

It's the stuff of reality TV. Who would have thought my life is supposed to
    be a fairy-tale?

Disney got it wrong. That pretty blonde gallivanting with Prince Phillip,
    singing of dreams, rainbows and sunshine, what a joke. That
    sanitized tale? My life? Oh, it's mostly right. I was a princess,

I was cursed, a fairy fucked up her gift, and I was raised in the forest with
    smiling animals and three lazy fat fairies. Disney even got the
    getting-pricked-by-a-spindle part right. I fell into a deathless
    sleep, and everyone else did too, except for that

dick of a prince, my hero, my husband, my rapist. See dear ones, that's the
    part that's left out. Princes are for rescuing damsels in distress, but
    also for sneaking in a quick fuck in between the finding and the
    rescuing. After all, it was true love's kiss that awoke me,

not true lust's fuck. No need to worry, will she think I'm good, will I
    please her? Nope, I was out cold, so why not? Typical college
    nightmare tale. Who would tell that story to their kids? Everyone
    has something to hide, Disney, the college, the parents, the
    skeletons in the closets.

Fast forward to the end, when I'm marrying the prince, oh that part's right.
    But the reality isn't far from Nick and Sandy's. Pregnancy – sweet
    sixteen, yes that's right, I'm a child bride too – and ready to pop.
    Now twins. Yes, twins, just what I always dreamed. It was a
    cover up, the whole marriage, a sham . . . Hide the rapist in
    legitimacy, society loves a

criminal who does right by his victim. Because, no one really gave a fuck
about what I thought. Oh our little darling has come back from
the grave, they said. Just smile, smile darling, as you dance away
to your wedding day.

We're all right, I suppose, locked into this fairytale world of cut corners
and neat little endings, that would make Grimm and his brother or
Andersen freak. So beware of spindles, beware of princes, beware
of fairies, hell, beware of the whole damn thing called Life.

Yellow
Sarah Galo

Yellow, I learned, was the color of lust.
Or has always been considered so by
The male poets. Look at Browning, Williams.

Dirty, dirty blondes.

I sat before the mirror, my golden hair,
A call to come, a flag of surrender,
A siren's song. Is this what I asked for?

When Miss Kubliek's long hair ceased to be an asset,
And became a burden, something for anxiety
To nest in, she cut her hair, and when asked
Why, answered, "It made me nervous."

Mine as well. I used to have a ritual, it never
Failed to make me pretty. I washed my hair
Only at night, so I could be beautiful. But
It was a ritual. A habit. An obsessive one,
And my hair grew tired and thin.

So it's not completely the fault of your
Waxing and waning gaze, pulling me
In with the tide, pushing me out with the
Tide. This modern siren now takes the knife,
And lets the yellow locks fall into her lap,
The sea.

Still a dirty, dirty blonde, but no longer a
Pretty one.

After
Sarah Gallo

Attractive. Being found attractive and being told after the anticlimax,
      after. After his hands slid under your shirt, around your
      Waist. After.

Another told me the same. After. After he quietly said there was
      Another girl. Then, he told me I was beautiful. Not just
      Attractive. Beautiful, so beautiful, and shouldn't I be
      Thankful, because good things will come to me.

Only after the fact. After we imitated post-coital positions.
      Or after we kissed. And most certainly after, *My dear,*
      I have something to tell you . . . but you are beautiful,
      I've always thought so, as you leave me.

Blues, or 'These few precious days, I'll spend with you'
Sarah Galo

Sing me a song, low and long,
slow and sad.

Unhinged,

I will shed my skin, remove the mud
from my eyes, and see you,

smoky and shy, a crooner out of place.

My ribs exposed, a house for my beat
and breath, I will glide, I will stare, I will undo
the locks of my hair,

spread out before you,
as you sing me a song.

Neruda
Sarah Galo

I miss you, without knowing how, or where or why.

Yes, I will rip the words from Neruda's lips, and place them on my page.
Change the order, and make them mine. Eliot said a good writer
never copies, a good writer steals.

I've had those words wandering through my head all day long, *I love you,*
without knowing how, or when or from where . . . and then
I saw you.

I heard a song, songs really. New and old, I wanted you. Again.

Even when your fingers traced over my lips, and your working hands held
mine, I knew, I knew. When we finally kissed, no longer
unknown, no longer . . .

A Final Scene in a Bar

Sarah Galo

The boundary of you and me, the boundary of us where you and I could
      not and should not trespass

When his eyes measure your legs, the length around his waist, your feet
      crossed at his hips

Crossed over the line between us, when an embrace between friends is no
      longer a simple good bye

When he invites you to late night diners, and even later night walks in the
      park, or rather playground,

chances to get metaphysical, an excuse to watch you as you watch the stars

      to watch your hands,

      your waist

      and hips,

      the way your lips move as you speak or sigh

kiss me and watch the world shatter, how much it matters, how much I
      now know sitting beside you flirting with ideas

from a year before

should't have done it, didn't want to admit it, but how I loved you,

      then, in the dining room,

      watching you talk,

      watching your mouth

and jaw,

sharply drawn figures

knowing I could love you, do anything for you, anything you asked

bend down/kneel down

and love you wrongly

lay beside you, kiss your scars and love you rightly;

we are perfect, and I remember this moment before it is completed,
before it is past

I see us sitting, wine and beer, laughing and I touch your arm,
and I am letting the wine

get to my head and the room is loud, but all I can hear is music
in another room, another night,

and I think you are going to put your arm around me, I feel
you move, I see your arm

move upward, behind my back and I feel, wanting to love,
love, love you

and I will remember this moment,

when I am in crowds,

when I am in love

when I am in bed

before it ends

On the Tappan Zee Bridge
Sarah Galo

Historically, each time in your car, we have spoken of,
naming and unnaming, diagnosing ourselves, of
my sadness or your gravitation to heights or sharp
objects or my medication, or yours. And always, always
as we cross the Tappan Zee, weaving through the traffic.
Repetition, knowing my mind will always go back to you,
to you, even when I have seen someone new.

You are safe, I know you. Safe and easy because there
will be no surprise, the conversation will be the same,
different names, different films, different times, but same
order, same essentials. But when you spoke

in the middle,"You are so beautiful, you are so beautiful,"
I believed you for the first time.

Facing It

Sarah Galo

I forget your face even as I look, I cannot picture it.

When we kiss, I know the outline of you, but when I speak,
        when I look away, when I sit in bed, and think of you,

I cannot see you, and there is compilation of faces instead, the features
        of others with yours. You are not the first.

You must forgive me, I lost myself three years ago, while I know myself,
        I do not, and forget what I look like, forget what I want.

After a Death
Sarah Galo

1.
She said, *I am unhooking my mind, and leaving it on the shelf*, afterwards.
        Could not think, could not bear it.

She saw his face everywhere. She decided, knew for fact, that if ten men
        were lined up in front of her, she could find half

reminded her of him. Half: one the cheekbones, another the eyes, yet
        another the lips. Composites of a god.

2.
She lay in bed, hands
reaching at empty space.

She threw it out, dragged
the king-sized mattress

to the street, left it to take
in the rain, went out

and bought a twin
mattress.

Single. Alone.

She could prop it
against the wall:

stare at the wall,
the blank wall, and
she could sleep,

eventually.

The outward space,
a reminder.

3.
Began running, began walking to work,
     walked miles and watched the leaves fall,

and then down; the sun hurt, bare-faced
     and naked without sunglasses.

Back to the bed at night, alone with the wall,
     white and empty: *remind me.*

Down. Back. Pull.
Sarah Galo

Down. I want to bring you down,
not ruin you,
just back. Back to earth.

Pull you down from your
precious pulsars, dying stars,
back to earth.

Down to life, pull you back from the
cold, fiery lab-coat world,
Back to the ruins, pull you down

into the muck and waste
left behind.

Alight

Imminent Summer

Bobby Texel

It starts
with that familiar sting;
the discovery
of the season's first sunburn,
continuing with
that familiar nighttime smell –
the damp scent
of a salty moisture in the air.
Sea? Sweat? Adventure?
It is difficult to pinpoint,
but is nonetheless intoxicating.
Even if a least favorite season,
the time between spring and fall
draws one in.

I Get What Edgar Was Talking About
Bobby Texel

When you are alone
with no one else near
and there are thoughts
that you want to share
you must go
and walk amongst the stones
and talk out loud
to those who are there,
but at the same time
are not.

Sometimes the best conversations
are the ones you can only imagine
and at least playing out your part
is enough to pull you through.

The dead are the best listeners.

An Examination
Bobby Texel

"A new lease on life" –
it is an interesting idiom.

Granted, it is nice to get something new –
but a new lease?

When you boil it down
new lease or not,
you still owe someone
your life.

I suppose it is nice to know
that you still have a lease at all
even if you might owe
someone else,
an accident,
a deity,
or a doctor.

The only way you can be sure
you are getting a good deal
is when you are both
the lessee and the lessor.

No Comfort

Humble Home
Sara Blevins

Step into my humble home, my simple dwelling place
Notice all my whitewashed walls, and paintings of your face
I'm seeking out the vengeance, with my quietly done hate
Turn your eyes from the blinding light of your empty, empty fate

I'm ready to receive you, so give it all to me
I'm trying to deceive you, quit pretending you can see
The dream in my brain, is the nightmare when I wake
I can't seem to get free from this hollow empty
I can't seem to get free, this shell that's trapping me

I taste you bleeding, though you are fine
I feel you smother when you breathe
Laying in your arms makes the whole world weightless
My fears subside, your love takes their place
Waves of still waters crash through my mind
Winds of calm storms rage from behind
You can isolate me from my world, you can't take us away

Time will take away the pain, who will stop the memories from coming
Waves of still waters crash through my mind
Winds of calm storms rage from behind
It's not as good as I'm remembering it to be, I'm making it mean more
than it ever did to me
A thirsting flame unquenchable
In even the height of desire and rage, against the burning.

Saturday

Sara Blevins

Saturday stays forever, but forever's just a day
Saturday whispers he'll never, ever go away
Saturday's joy is for me now, but I'm only at my turn
When forever's day is over, for my Saturday I'll yearn

I need the seventh day to keep me
I need the gently rolling hills
I need the saddest eyes I've ever seen
I need the winds on my ears
I don't think I have ever felt this way
So much that I am sure
I know I've never seen a Saturday, before

I need the seventh day to keep me; I need the breath from his lips
I need the saddest eyes I've ever seen; I need the touch of his fingertips
I can never feel this way again, so much that I am sure
That I know I've never seen a Saturday, before

I can't live without my seventh day
I can't make it if I try
And if I've ever spoken truer things
Then before this, they were lies
I need the saddest eyes I've ever seen to look at my face
And if I can't have Saturday
God take me from this place.

Serenity
Sara Blevins

Serenity – falling serenity, land beside me
Hold me, touch me, bring peace to me
Serenity – sweet lovely, I ask you again
Caress me sweet lovely, do what you can

Your child – your petal pink as black
Your child, sweet lovely serenity
Subside not – your meek one, see small one
Tiny you
Nurture, subside not
Tiny you

Serenity – he is small, part of you
Bed he's down, angels watch
He is you, asleep
Morning rise – sleepy small, hold his hand
Tiny you
Together ride – see him later, let his eyes kiss you goodbye

Hello small serenity – sweet lovely serenity, little lovely
He is serenity, sun in the sky, sun at night
Subside not you meek one
See small one, tiny you
Nurture you, subside not
Tiny you.

Not Ashamed
Sara Blevins

I'm not ashamed of my feelings,
Though there's nothing in my shell,
Knowledge is nothing, a no one
Invading me
Take my life away

I'm not ashamed of my fear,
Though it covers me like raindrops,
Emotions are the darkness, thieves
In the night

I'm not ashamed of my triumph,
Though it's grey on the white,
Love is the wind, touches your face
The moment that you feel it
Gone.

Stalking
Sara Blevins

Prowlers are watching me
When I dine and when I sleep
Feet on the ground, arms to the sky
Prowlers are holding and stretching me
Tall and wide and fast and fierce
This alliance
We are
Predators are stalking me
I crook my finger when I feel them
Fear
An aphrodisiac
I'm stretching and pulling and challenging
Words of wisdom
Flat notes of music
Authorities are watching me
Quiet volcano
When I move and when I stay
Threats
I'll guide them into my veins
Run through, pierce, puncture
My demons are watching me
When it's dark and when it's dusk
No light for my candle
No fuel for my lantern
Probe the walls

The Exchange
Sara Blevins

Sleepy little soul

Arms around his neck

Whiskers and sweat and dirt

Landscape

Concrete, gently bounce before little eyes

Confusion reaching behind her head

She can't see where those thoughts are

Voices

His laughter wants to bring comfort

Yet something doesn't feel like him

Loosening grasp, the hand off

Big people, exchanging unknown content

Filthy hands and fingers, tiny little bags

She is content

Her foggy mind

Watching him throw back glances

He walks away

Not going with him

A stranger's arms

Chimeras
Sara Blevins

Human head with eyes that die – inside a living face

Lips without language – a useless tongue

Legs that twitch and ache for freedom – defeated

Hair and skin – foreign to their bodies

Do I swim or do I fly or do I crawl

Medical waste

Hammers and scalpels - tranquilizers and sedatives

Flat earth theory is the habitat – for "those" crossbreeds

Puppy ears – kitten tails

Bird wings – soft underbellies

Scalpels

Tube

Tray

Cut

Poke

Observe

Measure

Dive

Sara Blevins

When I set my eyes on you,

My first time exclaimed – this woman is my fate,

When can I muster her infatuation,

Love drums its beat upon my heart – chemicals fire off,

When I first set my eyes on you – thoughts,

I wondered into Eden,

How would your hair smell – how would your hips taste,

I pictured locking us away,

A balcony with no escape,

I pictured us in the breeze – top story without reprieve,

Show me inside you,

You did down – burrow in my skin,

You chip away – scale my walls,

Oh my God you are beautiful,

Daze – dazed,

You are my maze – million piece puzzle,

Crystal scattering light,

Oh my God you are beautiful,

Lean back and dip my hair in you smell,

Favorite me, my darling,

Hold me as a treasure – fall with me,

Disregard the end,

Dive,

Dive with me my love – caress me my Goddess,

My lips,

Your lips.

Fragments
Sara Blevins

Exclusion

Inverse immersion

You're not one of us

Shifty eyes

Calculated replies

You scare us

Inside the lines

You force us out

Comfort abandoned

We can't handle you more

Remind us of feelings we avoid

What is your position for pain

Exclusion

Inverse immersion

Don't expose us

We hate that you're us

We're fragments

We're pieces

We're liars and layers

And hatred at best

Exclusion

Inverse immersion

Fault lines support us

Depleted foundations of safety

Tall – tall - tall - proud

Scared – ashamed – needful

frantic

Funeral

Sara Blevins

I went to a funeral once
I saw myself in the box
Tunnel vision held me tight
Inseparable as new lovers
I saw myself as a child
Running through the fields
Harnessing the power of imagination
No way was a wrong way
When my son was born
Death licked my ears
Creation pulls our life force
When I gave, I felt a pull
At the funeral, I saw a ghost
He stood over me
We held hands
He said that I was already gone, that I shouldn't fret
That he was my master, my lord
That I shouldn't fear the reaper
That I was
That I am
That I never had been

His Arms
Sara Blevins

He feels my aching, he is with me in my storms
My weakness and my fear and my trembling, are for him nothing
He is able more than me, he is stronger loving longer
His arms will never fail me

In those times that my mind just can't understand
On those days where no matter how hard I try, I cannot comprehend
I can't control the winds, though sometimes I know I can
When things won't go my way, when I feel they're out of hand

I am strengthened by my trials, even if I don't see it in them
My feelings try to tell me, that it's going on for miles
I ask for his help, my patience is wearing thin
After all is said and done, a figure standing tall

Even if I didn't feel it
Even if I didn't know it
He was with me through it all
He held me in his arms

Hoard

Sara Blevins

Risky hunger,
There's enough to go around.
Hoard
Keep
Hide
Dig the earth,
Submerge a bunker.
How long do you think that will last?
Primal lizard brains,
Animalistic sounds,
Hedonistic premonitions,
Gawking sexual obsessions,
Puppeteers pulling strings,
Faster primates grinning,
Cabbage soup nourishing,
Accept.
You will end.
Beg if you will, you will end.

I Don't Like to Touch
Sara Blevins

I don't like to touch

When your skin is near me

The energy, heat, and pain

I hunch my shoulders

The tension, racing, and aching

I'm a ball now

I'll roll away from you

You're so tender

You hurt me with your kindness

My fists to my temples

I'm invisible now

I'll hide from your view

Convex pools of compassion

Get out of my soul

The probing, undressing, longing, and love

Part me

It's the only time I can feel you

Numbing pleasure

Gasping

Dizzy

I don't like to touch

I am a raindrop now

I'll dry up

Pull away from you

If Hell is Peace
Sara Blevins

If Hell is dark, perhaps
If Hell is silent, peaceful
Maybe I'll fall
Maybe a leaf from a Maple tree
Bells
Sing for me bells
Crash against reality
Vie for my soul
Screams
Sweet salve for my numbness
They belong to me
Twist and grasp for the sides
They're never there
Loneliness
A welcome lover
Cover me
Black out
Black it all out
Never finish
Prayers go out on my behalf
Meanwhile
Float in disregard
Bask upon the waters of sorrow
No bright rays touch my skin
Perhaps Hell is peace
Maybe life is the lie
Speck
I am a speck

Jamie
Sara Blevins

Beautiful Jamie, such a long hard life
Lives by herself, locks her doors at night
Beautiful Jamie, will she ever be full
Takes her bath by candlelight, a wine glass by her side

Beautiful Jamie, arose from her long sleepless night
Beautiful Jamie, looked in the mirror and cried
Can you blame her, for the things she's done
Beautiful Jamie, just wants to be loved by someone

Beautiful Jamie, born and raised in her small town ways
Glamorous Jamie, lady of ladies
Who cannot love her, the light in her eyes
Lovely smile
Beautiful Jamie, give her a chance
Sit and talk for awhile

Beautiful Jamie, traveling out in her freshly painted car
Her maps by her side, waving goodbye
Going so far
Destination unknown for beautiful Jamie, could be anywhere
Beautiful Jamie, wherever you're going
I sure hope you get there

Liar
Sara Blevins

I have silenced my words for a long time now

I go around and around with myself

I am afraid of someone

Liar

You lie to yourself

You don't hurt anymore

Bullshit

You shove it down your throat so hard, that you choke on your own
    pretend complacency

Eating your sorrow

Drowning in causes and show

If it isn't sex, if it isn't food, if it isn't drugs

Medicate   .

You know why

When you actually let it out, you see it on paper

you feel suicidal with pain

you know what haunts you

you know there is no God

I see you looking around the room

Nanotech
Sara Blevins

Red wine in your mouth
Roaring thoughts
How long will you hold it in
Is it gathering the evidence
Then, the conclusion
You don't know what to feel
Who can you tell
Will they think you mad
In your mind, visions
Noises
Industrial music pushing against suburban background
Stranglehold, stomping on everything natural
Will you be a beast or a man
Are you a beast now
Without nothing left but elevation
Climb the Tower of Babel
Open yourself
Punctuation is finality
Spit and twirl
And a single light
Hold up your fate
Do you see anything

No Such Apocalypse

Sara Blevins

No such Apocalypse
No concept of time
No pressure – no hurry – no need
Only our feeble constructs
Many can't conform
Homeless – jobless – alone – phantoms
No such ending
Nothing revolves around us
We don't matter – we don't care - not the nucleus
Thought in the various fields
Volley
Theories bucking theories
Ideas warring for position
No such apocalypse
Flutes play our song
We are all Greece
We are a dark spot
We don't exist – we are a black hole – she'll turn her eyes from us

On He Walked
Sara Blevins

He couldn't stand to see this world,
So he kept his eyes to the ground ahead,
Down the street and around the corner,
And away from the world and on he walked,

Pass Edith in her rocking chair,
Knitting blankets for her bed,
Memories fading away from her,
She's so cold since John's been dead,

Coming up on little Timmy,
Playing sand pile with his trucks,
Can't go back inside alone,
That's what mommy says since his daddy's drunk,

A limping dog is hobbling by,
A scar is where there is no eye,
Whimpering as he's coming near,
Can't help the fear he feels inside,

Here's Diana's lonely house,
No trespassing signs hang on the fence,
Danny has threatened to come back again,
Poor Diana hasn't spoken since,

Colonel Andy's house is full of people,
Young and old and all alike,
Until the dawn has come again,
The party will rage on tonight.

Secrets Best Kept
Sara Blevins

He thought about his shortcomings
Dwelled upon his spite
Loathing and faults made him up
He tasted like vinegar to you
He pushed out his imperfections
Yet you rejected
He fought for your attention
And blended into your respite
He dreamed of a moment of taste
Wanted to be your salt
The seasons to your years
And found himself nowhere to you
He purged his imperfections
Isolated your discontents
He threw himself into your fire
All to be your muse
Your admired form
Not enough
No matter his trials
Rejection
Imperfection
Never admit you long for him
Never admit that you fret
Never embrace him
Never your pet
Crush him to save you
Secrets best kept

Spirit Astray
Sara Blevins

Leaving the flesh

Going away

Pulling apart

Spirit astray

Thin soft chord

Anchor us down

Lightshows in heaven

Colors abound

Nothing is solid

Bolted or real

Cautionary tales

Won't let us see

Fabric of time

Lies of the solid

In dreams we're there

Days slice our fate

Fiction is written

Algorithm of reality

Space and force

Bow our heads

Don't look up

Restraint is the key

Hide

Tremble

Spiral staircase

Rocking chair

Move, but never go anywhere

Lies

DAISY

Emily Williams

It was the last time they saw Paris.
Her wide-brimmed hat and an old floral dress,
His studded leather belt,
And there was fire in their eyes.

Until he said the spark will never
Come from an unlit candle.
But she told him he is the match,
So strike a flame.

Blown away with the leaves of August,
The feeling ever-so-present
Yet buried underneath the ground,
Just below the spring daisies.

He and his new shadow crush
The flowers to the floor.
She gets up and turns her head,
No tears anymore.

She is in New England,
Her wide-brimmed hat, a new dress
And a match in one hand,
Off to light another flame.

HOME
Emily Williams

I stare into endless brown eyes.
Long eyelashes, dark hair.
Ran my fingers over your face,
Trying to memorize you by heart.
We sat down in the shade
In the month of May,
Cried your feelings had strayed;
They had begun to decay.

Darling,
Here's to our fictitious future.
Swallow those drugs and swallow that liquor.
Down it goes, you'll find a cure.
But there's something I must reassure.
Your new found love is premature.
She's with you 'cause she feels secure.

Two weeks was all you needed.
I can see that you seem happy.
She's another for your eyes to feed.
I just hope you're really fucking happy.
I won't stick around; I know you'll just feel sorry.
So go be with that girl,
Take her heart; fill it up in a hurry.
It'll be over soon enough one day.

Sunshine,
Here's to our fictitious future.
Swallow those drugs and swallow that liquor.
Down it goes, you'll find a cure.
There's something I must reassure.
Your new found love is premature.
She's with you 'cause she feels secure.

You were my lovely, my ugly, and my best friend
You were my first, my last, and my descend
You fucked it all.
Act like you could never love again.
Yet with intent you grab her hand.
Made me go perfectly insane.
Is there something I don't understand?

Baby,
Here's to our fictitious future.
Swallow those drugs and swallow that liquor.
Down it goes, you'll find a cure.
There's something I must reassure.
Your new found love is premature.
Don't waste your time being with her.

Two weeks was all you needed.
I can see that you seem happy.
She's another for your eyes to feed.
I hope you're real fucking happy.
You're all that I've got,
Yet I hate you with all I have.
I don't want to let you go.
So, please, don't let me go.

I try to spit out every hate.
Life's a bitch,
And she is too,
But what would happen if you knew,
That I cannot stop loving you.

FLUTTER
Emily Williams

There they go again
Fluttering their wings
Every time

Every dream
Every thought
Every word

They flutter
Spread their wings
But never fly away

Years will race by
Hours will drag
But nothing

Nothing
Will stop the feeling
That takes ahold

Deep beneath
The surface
In between time
And space

Nestled by heart
And soul
It holds a home
There forever

Somewhat a burden
There to remind
Of the pain of
Absence

Gone forever to the eye
Never to return to the arms
But the feeling is never more present
The flutter, the ever so familiar

Flutter of love.

THE ART OF LIES
Emily Williams

Entangled in the thorns, inescapable
Crushes all life on its twisted way out
Can't reach, the ever-dimming light retreating
Only leads to a fall far deeper than the first

The words flow from your mouth with such ease
From your lips, swiftly, it flows through the air
Swirls above your head and through the night sky
Back to the ears of those caught in the stem

Narrowly escaped its desperate grasp
With every fall down, there's another step up
Never again to be marked with the stamp
The proof that shows I'm just like the rest

Time only spills the remains of the thorns
Hands can't turn back the deception once spoke
No matter the desirous spirit that lurks
What's done is done, and no more can be said.

Nighttime Flood
Emily Williams

Nighttime Flood.

Darkness seeped over the town,
Spilling onto the pavement,
Drowning the sun's last fight.

Power Outage.

The old man in the cottage
Swims through the murky hallway
In search of a match to light.

Tide of Darkness.

A woman has lost her glasses
In the saturated room.
No more reading for the night.

Washing Over.
The town is drained of last hopes
So they dive into their beds
Awaiting something bright.

Nighttime Flood.

Overflowing
Emily Williams

Overflowing. My soul is on a rampage endlessly streaming surges and urges of beauty and fury from the stage in my brain out onto sweet lips.

Glowing. In my lover's eyes, his nasal passage breathing in and out the sound of music into the soul of the world.

Growing. Can you feel it? Roots shooting down beneath our sneakers, owing our inevitability to the earth.

Knowing. It is nothing but here and now, we give ourselves back to the universe. There are stars in everything and everyone.

Rifles
Emily Williams

Rifles, knives, nukes, and fighting
Clouded sense of freedom lingers in my mind
Evil is rising and monsters start biting
A glimmer of hope is so hard to find

Clouded sense of freedom lingers in my mind
Gunman stationed at twelve o'clock
A glimmer of hope is hard to find
Stuck in a cage yet to be unlocked

Gunman stationed at twelve o'clock
What's left in the world but hate and greed
Stuck in a cage left to be unlocked
Fulfilling the wants and not any needs

What's left in the world but hate and greed
Money. Oh money, the leading cause of death
Fulfilling the wants and not any needs
Millions of souls forced to take their last breath

Money. Oh money, the leading cause of death
Give a man a uniform and a gun. He will kill.
Millions of souls forced to take their last breath
People living lives only power can fulfill

Imagination
Emily Williams

Imagination dead, no hope for salvation
Chained to the desk, glued to a book
Molding straight into society's creation

Fine specimens to add to their fixation
Remove the skull, extract the remains
Imagination dead, no hope for salvation

Boy grows up with parental deprivation
No one there to soothe his childhood pains
Trying to mold to society's creation

Loveless, he works in a big corporation
Failed to break free of his own restraints
Imagination dead, no hope for salvation

No wonder he has all of this frustration
Forced into cuffs; numbness takes over
A failure of society's creation

He knew it was eternal damnation
Just one shot, one fatal desperation
There he killed society's creation
Imagination dead, no hope for salvation

Beware the Insurgent

Demons
Evan McCracken-Iverson

I can tell from your blood stained hands that you've given in. Those demons knocking on your door, you just let them in. You've let the enemy win yet again and it saddens me to see your wrists indented.

Bad Chains
Evan McCracken-Iverson

Whenever I talk about slavery I have bad dreams. This race getting hung up and looked at like art in their gallery. We brag about chains now, but people used to live in them.

Scars whipped across bodies, people taken without looking back. It's sad that this is a fact, and matter of fact, it should not have happened.

We should not have to learn about such things but I guess that's history, right? Books battered with false hope like their backs.

MLK had a dream, but all it led to was nightmares.

Sunshine
Evan McCracken-Iverson

As soon as you came into my life my days went from dark cloud dull grey
to sun shining bright sun rays.

You are the drug to my addiction, you are the light to my darkness,
you stopped this infliction,
now I know where my heart is.

Lust
Evan McCracken-Iverson

The scent of you still lingers on these bed sheets.

I wait for the next time our lips meet again and I can feel your skin, even though I embrace you from within.

I had been taught that one day I would grow up and find the other half of me, which would make me complete. Now I'm not fully grown by any means, but I think I've found that person already.

What I mean would be you, sitting there, thick thighs, curly hair, hazel eyes do not compare to the way my feelings sit above my heart.

Do I tell you how I really feel or will that drive you away? Or do I put the brakes on my heart and make it stay? And if you do end up feeling the same, where do we go from there?

I know you're going to a place far away from here soon. The past has taught me that it is hard to live in the present when you know there is no future.

So I am contemplating starting something I know I cannot finish.

2 AM Thoughts

Evan McCracken-Iverson

I loved you more than I could love myself. That one summer night, I still remember it like it was yesterday.

The way the street lights flickered by your house, the smell of wet grass from the storm the night before.

Right when I walked into your room, I was greeted by the sweet smell of your perfume on the dresser and clean sheets. After the lights shut off, the brightest conversations came out.

We were talking about our future, as your head was on my heart. I said that all I could ever dream of is being with you. Forever, you said nothing sounded better. Hearing that made my heart do jumping jacks.

You are my 2 AM thoughts but every time we were together at 2 AM I could not seem to think straight.

Everything seemed perfect until the floor boards above started to creak, I started to get scared, you were scared, we, we were scared . . . Scared that the imminent was about to happen.

I looked up at you, you looked down on me and when our pupils locked I knew it was over. Silence. What we have, or rather had was never going to be the same.

We were ruined. Ruined not by choice but by mistakes, ruined by the noise of that voice echoing down the stairwell. I shouldn't have been there, we both knew that, but you still let me in.

Shows that love can be blinding. I ran through love tornadoes for you, but I guess you forgot there was an I in the middle. I was in the middle, in the middle of you and your parents. They said that you were too young to love, but I knew that was not true, the feeling you gave me were anything but false.

We had too much planned for it to just be a blueprint. We already had a rough draft, but I forgot to edit out the run-on sentence because I never wanted it to end.

I hope you are doing just as great as I am; you recently asked what's wrong with me and I now know that it was you. I hope you find your true love, because my 2 AM thoughts now consist of someone that is not you.

21 Gun Salute

Evan McCracken-Iverson

The person I once knew does not exist anymore. You were my lifesaver, but even they disappear after some time, the sweet sound of hearing your name is bitter now.

The fresh smell of coffee in the morning. Decaf with two cups of cream, that's how you liked it, right?

I remember that one day when you said I'm proud of you. How did you see in me what no one else has?

When those 3 shots from 7 soldiers fired off, that 21 gun salute, I cried. Crying shows weakness but these rivers of emotions that run down my face, just like the ones we used to fish are stronger than ever.

You have made me what I am today and I just wish you could see that. I wish you could know the reason I write is because of you.

Premeditated Mass Murder
Evan McCracken-Iverson

When I woke up the day was as normal as it's ever been, little did I know the world would be changed forever by the end of it.

I didn't know planes were supposed to fly into buildings, Dad. "It was an accident," he said. 17 minutes had passed and a second accident had happened.

Fire shooting out of those buildings like a breath from a dragon's mouth, people jumping out of windows leaving widows; hoping to get saved from below.

I had never seen so many people upset over an "accident." I later learned that this accident was planned, premeditated mass murder.

Reality Check

The Fiend

Danielle Corcione

I am Gothic and a romantic,
a man-made monster
and a "deliberate decision"

I could've been your Adam,
but a fallen angel instead
bring my vessels to life

concocted by you,
that was created by a woman
only eighteen years of age

we are the living fiction
for the audience to read,
and the critics to rate

we are the nightmare
of a doctor's reality
and a daughter's pen

Alpha Waves

Danielle Corcione

In my bed,
I am falling into fantasy,
face down, plummeting into my pillow.

I am dreaming to escape reality,
and escaping reality to dream and contemplating,
brainstorming,
things I'll forget by morning.

Graduation

Danielle Corcione

a bittersweet call
of Pomp and Circumstance
that echoes like the wind,
a memory within a picture.

soon the school band
will chant a Recessional song,
the brass ensemble like a church choir.

today's hymn will become
tomorrow's nostalgia.
the teenage years filled with misery,
we will forget,
in years, to remember the times
as if they were golden.

Sincerely, Jill
Danielle Corcione

Your thick rimmed glasses,
striped sweater, black peacoat,
and white SUV from '98.

It's been over a year,
and I thought I'd never want you back,
but now I see, I can't find the perfect man,
because I can't have you.

I can't have your intellect,
or your dry humor,
in my life ever again.
Never.

The messages you don't answer.

The songs I will not play,
I cannot play,
that I would play.

What's Your Fortune?

Danielle Corcione

an unlucky day
for a lucky fellow

Friday the 13th
was the date
my dad got struck by lightning

and lived.

1500 Miles Away
Danielle Corcione

The walls were turquoise
when I woke from unsettling dreams
to a Spanish sitcom with English subtitles.

My right arm was connected
to a clear bag of fluids
of what I was told was,
"agua y penicilina."

A middle-aged woman asked,
"porque no estas duirmiendo?"
and I blinked at her
while she injected another syringe
into my left arm.

My eyelids grew heavy,
but I then fear the feeling of sleep
while the Bachacha music faded
with the credits on the TV screen.

Roar

Danielle Corcione

outside the ocean waves roared, and Jeanette heard their melody from her
bedside. the clock ticked a quarter to seven, but she's already
late for work. water dripped off of Richard's dresser. the bouquet
of crimson roses fell over, but the vase wasn't broken. "I'm
leaving you," was all he said as he packed his final bag.

the roar wasn't the door slam, but the shatter of the glass frame on the
nightstand. it was a photograph taken the first time she laid eyes
on the horizon of the kite beach. it wasn't long after she
remembered saying, "let's just not go back." a line she'd recite at
her wedding reception.

she thought her dream of living in Cabarete with the love of her life left
with the roar of his plane. that was about sixteen years ago, but
she's still in love. her love was not the one she traveled to
paradise with, but paradise itself.

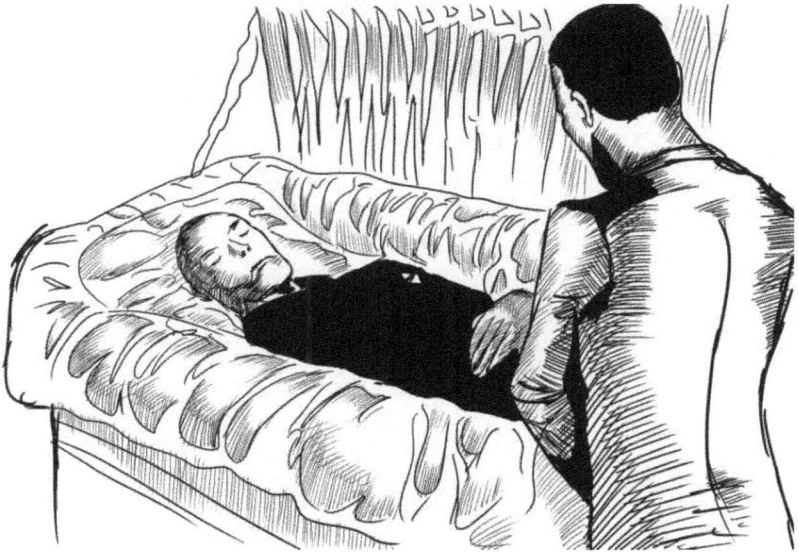

Me?

(DO YOU)

Craig Harrison

DO YOU HELP?
DO YOU CARE?
ARE YOU ALWAYS THERE?

DO YOU CRY?
DO YOU SCREAM?
DO YOU AT THE VERY LEAST TRY?

DO YOU PROMOTE LOVE AND HAPPINESS?
OR DO YOU EXPRESS HATE AND SADNESS?
DO YOU CARE ABOUT YOUR NEIGHBOUR?
DO YOU FORGIVE YOUR ENEMY?

DO YOU PUT OTHERS FIRST?
DO YOU GIVE UP YOUR TIME?
DO YOU EARN MONEY FOR OTHERS?
DO YOU RESPECT A STRANGER?

DO YOU
I'LL ASK AGAIN
DO YOU?

DO YOU PUT YOURSELF FIRST?
OR DO YOU HELP OTHERS?
DO YOU LOVE ALL LIFE?
OR DO YOU ONLY LOVE THE LIFE CLOSEST TO YOU?

Greatest battle

Craig Harrison

So many battles you have won
but sadly you won't win this one.
The battle that we will all face one
day THE BATTLE OF TIME

Forget the tyrants and the terrorists
the greatest enemy to our survival is time.
From the moment of our births, we are entered into this battle
THE BATTLE OF TIME

We know so little, but we know it is meant to be
time will come and time will go
but the memories shall not
time will continue to flow

War after war, billions after billions
but the war we should be fighting
the battle we should be entering
THE BATTLE OF TIME

Can not see

Craig Harrison

So dark, so very dark
but I hear a voice
and I can feel a breeze
but I don't know where I am
all I know is that I'm alone surrounded by people

I can hear people calling my name
Since I lost my sight nothing is the same

I didn't just lose my vision, I lost so much more
My independence
my job
my confidence
my self-esteem
I will never get to live my childhood dream

It's hard to only see one colour for the rest of time
BLACK
no colour, just
BLACK

Who else cries

Craig Harrison

It's always bad news that we read
even worse news that we hear
it's enough to make you run in fear.

War after war
death after death
Every second a life-form is taking its final breath

The 6th commandment says thou shall not kill
but not only do we still do, some even do it for a frill
Every life that dies, every final breath that is taken
makes me sad and angry that I can not save them

My love for life includes the biggest and the smallest
Alien, human, bugs or birds
no discrimination on who or what I love
so when one dies, I question who else cries.

Something or nothing
Craig Harrison

What will I see when I arrive?
What will people feel when I leave?
Will I see red or will I see white?
Will I be walking into the dark or the light?

I had a beginning, and one day I will have an end,
but hopefully I still have a long time to go
even if time is beginning to show.

But I can not help but feel intrigued about what comes after
Will there be screams or tears of laughter?

Or

Maybe there is nothing once we die
except for our loved ones to have a good cry.

je crains (I fear)

Craig Harrison

I fear that no one will remember
I fear that I will be forgotten
When I die who will care

I have this fear
and it makes me scared
is my life meaningless
I fear no one will care

When I'm gone will my life live in memory
will my personality be remembered
will people even care about my history

I fear no one will remember
I fear that I will be forgotten

———————————

Je crains que personne ne se souviendra
Je crains que je vais oublié
Quand je mourrai, qui prendra soin

J'ai cette peur
et ça me fait peur
est ma vie vide de sens
Je crains personne ne se souciera

Quand je suis parti sera ma vie vivre dans la mémoire
sera ma personnalité se rappeler
les gens vont s'occuper même de mon histoire

Je crains personne ne se souviendra
Je crains que je vais oublié

A sole destroying friendship
Craig Harrison

You give and I take
but it's all your crap
if I was anyone else they would give you slap

I'm not sure why we're friends
yet I remain until our life ends
9 years and counting
but when I'm with you, sometimes if feels like I'm drowning

I'm a good person and I forgive you
but you push me to the point where I wish I could say this friendship is
through

I search the world

Craig Harrison

I search the world looking for peace
all I find is a world at war.
From North to South and East to West
All I see is what the human race does best
They kill, they cheat and lie
but everyone I ask doesn't know why.

I search the world looking for love
but I have no such luck,
They say they love they say they care
but come my death bed they are not there
I've begun to question if love is real
If not ,then what is it I feel.

I search the world and all I see
is no one quite like me
I see beauty and I see hate
but no one quite like me, to date.

I search the world looking for you
but I can not see, I can not find.
From North to South and East to West
I search the world doing my best.

Depression

Craig Harrison

Every night when I lie down in bed
I begin to think what life would be like if i was dead
when i think of this I can't help but cry
for some reason i don't want to die

There are days when I have fun,
but I just watch TV, that's all I have ever done
I just don't want to go
but at this moment I feel so low

I have no idea what to do
I don't like my life but I don't want to die too

What is seen

Craig Harrison

Corner of my eye I catch a glimpse
And days go by until I see
There's no light, only darkness trapped in your mind, fighting to be free

All you feel is fear, sadness and sorrow
how long until your heart is hollow

Time gone by I knew you
Like the Devil and God
A battle is to be won
And the world will know when it is done

Once I saw hope in your eyes
Now sadness is all that I feel
Too far gone for your heart to heal

The soul is dying
As all the tears are drying

The world around is killing you
Nothing left, you can do

I want to save you from the fate install
which is harder than a wall

What I see in your eyes
As the image becomes clearer
Is my reflection, in the mirror

Because

Craig Harrison

I don't care about your age
or the fact you earn a higher wage
I love you because

Because when I see you I like how I feel
I love you because when I'm with you everything is real

I love your blond hair
and how much you love and care
I love your smile and your big hazel eyes
I love you because you're wise

I love you because you are smart
I love you because you remind me of art
so beautiful, the world must see
I love you because for some reason you love me

I love everything about you
and I'm happy you love me too

X

What am I?

Craig Harrison

When you say I'm not a proper man, what am I then?
I read and write, I like poetry and I like romance
I might not like fighting or drinking like most men
But I'm not ashamed to admit that I have feelings and I'm not scared
to express them

I like to watch ballet and listen to Opera
I like a bit of Mozart and some Beethoven
one of my favourites is Pachelbel's Canon in D
I think it's right when a man gets down on his knee

I believe in love, princes and princesses
I watch films like The Notebook and The Lake House
I like walks on the beach and watching the sun set
and I get scared when I come in contact with a threat

I like antiques and museums
I like art and shopping
So I might not be the same as other men
but if I'm not a proper man what am I then

I like football, I like fast cars
I want to take a trip to the planet Mars
I don't like cleaning, I've never had my nails done
I like women and I've always wondered what it'd be like to shoot a gun

So if I'm not a proper man, what am I then?

www.ingramcontent.com/pod-product-compliance
Lightning Source LLC
Chambersburg PA
CBHW032008040426

42448CB00006B/531